America's Leaders

THE CHIEF JUSTICE
of the Supreme Court

by Heather DeJohn

BLACKBIRCH®
PRESS

THOMSON
★
GALE

San Diego • Detroit • New York • San Francisco • Cleveland • New Haven, Conn. • Waterville, Maine • London • Munich

Photo credits: cover background, back cover, pages 3, 7, 8, 10, 13, 14, 15, 16, 17, 18, 20, 22, 25, 26, 28-29, 30-31, 32 © Creatas; Supreme Court cover inset © Corel; Jay cover inset, Warren cover inset, Rehnquist cover inset, pages 4, 5, 6, 7, 8, 9, 12, 14, 15, 16, 17, 18, 20, 21, 22, 23, 24, 26, 27 © CORBIS; pages 28-29 © Dover Publications

LIBRARY OF CONGRESS CATALOGING-IN-PUBLICATION DATA

DeJohn, Heather.
    The Chief Justice of the Supreme Court / by Heather DeJohn.
        p. cm. — (America's leaders series)
    Includes index.
    Summary: Takes a thorough look at the Chief Justice of the United States Supreme Court, including the history of the office, how the work relates to that of other government offices, and how Chief Justices have handled crises.
    ISBN 1-56711-663-9
    1. United States. Supreme Court—Officials and employees—Juvenile literature. 2. Judges—United States—Juvenile literature. [1. United States. Supreme Court—Officials and employees. 2. Judges.] I. Title. II. Series.
    KF8742.Z9 D45 2003
    347.73'2634—dc21   2002003524

Printed in United States
10 9 8 7 6 5 4 3 2 1

Table of Contents

The Leader of the Supreme Court

More than 200 years ago, a group of men wrote a document, the U.S. Constitution, which established the American government. The authors of the Constitution divided the government into 3 separate branches with equal powers. The legislative branch was made up of the Senate and the House of Representatives. The executive branch was led by the president. Finally, the judicial branch made up the nation's court system, with the Supreme Court as the highest court.

Under the Constitution, the legislative branch creates the nation's laws. The executive branch has the responsibility of putting the laws into action and making sure they are carried out.

Sometimes, however, people disagree about what a law means or if it is acceptable under the U.S.

The U.S. Constitution established the judicial branch of government.

Chief Justice William Rehnquist administered the oath of office to Bill Clinton in 1993.

Constitution. To settle disputes, they ask the Supreme Court to interpret the law. On those occasions, the judicial branch has powers that the other branches do not. As the nation's highest court, the Supreme Court decides whether the nation's laws follow the Constitution. If a law goes against the Constitution, the Supreme Court can rule that the law is unconstitutional. This power held by the Supreme Court is called judicial review.

USA FACT

In 2001, the chief justice's annual salary was $186,300 a year.

In some cases, a Supreme Court ruling means that a law must be rewritten or thrown out. In other cases, a ruling leads to a change, or amendment, to the Constitution.

5

The Supreme Court has 9 judges, or justices. The leader of the justices is the chief justice of the Supreme Court, and the other 8 justices are known as associate justices. The chief justice is the highest judicial officer in the nation.

Over the course of its history, the Supreme Court has made decisions that have affected the lives of every American citizen. The chief justice's most important responsibility is summed up by the words written above the main entrance to the Supreme Court Building: "Equal justice under law."

The 9 justices of the Supreme Court pose before their opening session in 1991.

What the Constitution Says

The Constitution states "the judicial power of the United States shall be vested in one Supreme Court." The document does not say that the court must have a chief justice.

Chief Justice John Marshall

The first act of the first Congress, however, was the Judiciary Act of 1789. This act stated that the Supreme Court would be made up of a chief justice and 5 associate justices. The act also divided the nation into 13 judicial districts. Those districts were organized into 3 circuits—the eastern, middle, and southern. Finally, the act gave federal courts the power to review the actions and legal decisions of state governments. In 1803, Chief Justice John Marshall decided a case known as *Marbury v. Madison.* This established the power of the court to interpret laws according to the U. S. Constitution.

USA FACT

The number of Supreme Court justices varied until 1869, when an act of Congress set the number at 9: a chief justice and 8 associate justices.

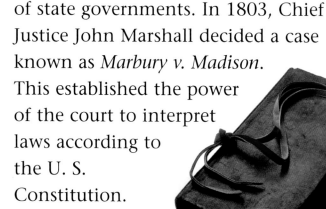

Becoming Chief Justice

The Constitution does not list requirements for becoming chief justice. All chief justices, however, have been lawyers with experience in presenting cases. Many justices have also had experience as judges in lower courts. Some justices have served in Congress or been cabinet members in the executive branch before sitting on the court.

All justices of the Supreme Court must be nominated by the president. The person nominated—the nominee—then appears before the Senate Judiciary Committee to be interviewed. If the committee votes to approve the nominee, the Senate then votes to confirm or reject. Presidents usually try to appoint justices who share their political opinions. That way, the justices may be more likely to make decisions with which the president agrees.

Retiring Chief Justice Warren Burger administered the oath of office to incoming Chief Justice William Rehnquist in 1981.

Chief Justice Warren Burger administered the oath of office to Sandra Day O'Connor, the first woman to serve on the Supreme Court.

The process of becoming chief justice is the same as for becoming a justice. The Senate can turn down a president's choice for chief justice. That happened for the first time in 1795, when the Senate rejected George Washington's nominee for chief justice, John Rutledge. Washington had appointed Rutledge to be acting chief justice. He assumed that Congress would follow his wishes and confirm Rutledge. Congress, however, did not agree with the president's choice. Rutledge served the shortest term of any chief justice, less than a year.

Responsibilities of the Chief Justice

The main job of the chief justice is to work with the associate justices to hear cases and make rulings on them. Each year, more than 7,000 petitions, or requests, are filed for the Supreme Court to hear cases. Reviewing the petitions takes up almost all of the court's time. The Court agrees to hear only about 100 cases per year. The justices usually choose cases they believe are most important. These are cases that most strongly affect the interpretation of the Constitution or that affect the lives of the greatest number of people.

The chief justice leads the meetings in which the justices decide on the cases they will hear. Justices discuss each petition and then vote on whether to accept it. The chief justice casts the first vote. The associate justices then cast their votes in order of their length of service on the Supreme Court.

Most cases selected by the justices have already been heard in lower courts, such as a state court or a U.S. district court. The person or group who loses such a lower court case may appeal—ask the next higher court to review the decision. Many times, appeals work their way up through the court system before they reach the Supreme Court.

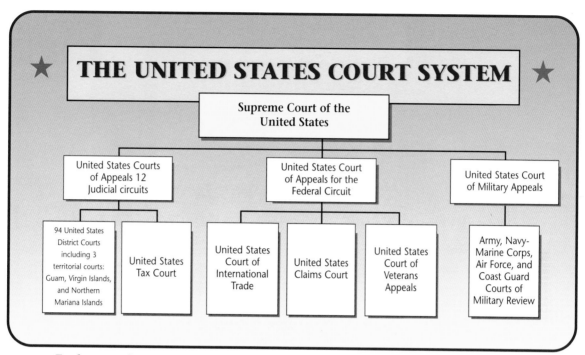

THE UNITED STATES COURT SYSTEM

Supreme Court of the United States

United States Courts of Appeals 12 Judicial circuits
United States Court of Appeals for the Federal Circuit
United States Court of Military Appeals

94 United States District Courts including 3 territorial courts: Guam, Virgin Islands, and Northern Mariana Islands

United States Tax Court

United States Court of International Trade

United States Claims Court

United States Court of Veterans Appeals

Army, Navy-Marine Corps, Air Force, and Coast Guard Courts of Military Review

Each year, the Supreme Court hears about 100 cases that have made their way through the federal court system.

Other Jobs

The Constitution does not describe the duties of the chief justice. Congressional acts over the years, however, have given the chief justice the job of overseeing any presidential impeachment trial in the Senate. An impeachment occurs when a president is accused of a crime. If the House of Representatives votes to impeach the president, he is then tried in the Senate. This has happened twice in American history.

In the U.S. Senate, Chief Justice William Rehnquist was sworn in before the impeachment trial of President Bill Clinton.

In 1868, Chief Justice Salmon P. Chase presided at the impeachment trial of President Andrew Johnson. In 1998, Chief Justice William Rehnquist presided over the impeachment trial of President Bill Clinton. Neither president was removed from office.

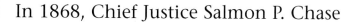

USA FACT

Traditionally, the chief justice also administers the oath of office to the incoming president and vice president at their inauguration ceremony.

The chief justice has additional powers and responsibilities as part of his job. As the spokesperson for the Supreme Court, he writes a yearly report about the activities of the Court as well as a review of the lower courts. The chief justice also oversees the Court's budget. Since these tasks can take a great deal of time, the chief justice appoints court officers, such as the administrative assistant and the public information officer, to assist him. The chief justice also has lawyers who serve as law clerks to help gather legal information and do research for various cases.

The Courtroom Hearing

A Supreme Court session is called a "sitting." On those days, the justices enter the courtroom by stepping out from 3 burgundy curtains behind the bench—the raised platform where they sit.

As they enter, the marshal of the Court introduces them by announcing, "The Honorable, the Chief Justice and the Associate Justices of the Supreme Court of the United States." The marshal calls the courtroom to order by calling "Oyez, oyez, oyez," (pronounced "o-yay"), which means, "hear ye." He continues, "All persons having business before the

Cameras are not allowed in the courtroom while the Supreme Court is in session, but official courtroom artists are allowed to draw a sitting.

Honorable, the Supreme Court of the United States, are admonished to draw near and give their attention, for the Court is now sitting."

14

People who are unhappy with Supreme Court rulings sometimes protest outside the Court.

Unlike many court cases, there are no witnesses or juries in Supreme Court trials. Once justices select a case, they prepare for the sitting by reviewing the evidence, testimony, and rulings from the original trials.

Visitors can attend Supreme Court sittings, although space is limited, and lines to enter the courtroom can be very long if the case is one that has gained a lot of attention. The courtroom presentation of a case has a time limit of one hour. Lawyers on each side of the case are allowed 30 minutes to present their arguments. The lawyers use this time to try to persuade the justices to agree with their point of view. During the lawyers' speeches, the justices sometimes interrupt to ask questions.

USA FACT

Each Supreme Court term begins on the first Monday in October and ends the following June. By the middle of May, the justices have heard the final cases of the term. For the rest of the term, they meet in the courtroom on Mondays at 10:00 to announce their rulings.

After the Sitting

After the courtroom sitting, the justices gather privately to discuss the case. Similar to the meetings that decide whether to take a case, the chief justice shares his ideas first. The associate justices follow in order of seniority. The justices discuss both sides of the case, and each justice decides which side he or she agrees with. Then the justices cast their votes. A majority of 5 votes is needed to decide the outcome of a case. The vote of the chief justice carries no more weight than the vote of any other justice. Chief justices have often been on the losing—or dissenting—side of a Court decision.

Next, the justices write opinions that explain their decision. Most often, one justice who voted with the majority writes the majority opinion. A justice who disagreed with the majority vote writes the minority, or dissenting, opinion. If a chief justice has voted with the majority, he may write the majority opinion himself. He can also assign that opinion to an associate justice.

USA Fact

Five people have served as both associate justice and chief justice: John Rutledge, Edward D. White, Charles Evans Hughes, Harlan F. Stone, and William H. Rehnquist.

Chief Justice Rehnquist poses in his chambers.

Supreme Court justices must clearly explain the reasons for a decision. Writing an opinion takes a great deal of time, because justices often have to explain earlier cases that have influenced their decisions. Once an opinion is written, justices who voted together work as a team to revise the opinion until they agree on the wording. Sometimes an opinion is rewritten more than 10 times.

Where Does the Chief Justice Work?

The Supreme Court Building is located in Washington, D.C. It is across the street from the U.S. Capitol, where Congress meets. Construction on the building was completed in 1935. Until that time, the Supreme Court did not have its own building. It was allowed to meet

The old Supreme Court chamber, in the Capitol, was used until 1935.

The Supreme Court Building is located across the street from the Capitol.

in an unused chamber of the Capitol. In 1929, Chief Justice William Howard Taft convinced Congress to set aside funds for the construction of a Supreme Court building.

The white marble structure is now one of Washington's best known landmarks. Each of the bronze entrance doors to the Supreme Court weighs over 6 tons and is covered by images of historic scenes. The main corridor of the building, the Great Hall, features sculptures of the former chief justices. The Court Chamber, where cases

The nine justices will gather together before proceeding to the Court Chamber to hear a case.

are heard, is located at one end of the Great Hall. This room features a raised bench behind which the justices sit while they are hearing cases. The chief justice sits in the center, with 4 associate justices to his left and right. The marshal of the Court sits to the right of the bench. Lawyers stand behind a lectern to

USA FACT

In September 2001, the Supreme Court was forced to meet away from the Supreme Court Building for the first time since it opened. Anthrax—a deadly bacteria—had been mailed to various government offices. Security officers found traces of anthrax in the Court mail room and closed the Court until the entire building could be inspected for the bacteria and cleaned.

make their speeches. This is directly in front of the chief justice's seat. The courtroom also has seats for visitors and news reporters.

The chief justice spends a great deal of time in his office, also called his chambers. In this office, he does paperwork and works on opinions. For conferences, the chief justice and associate justices meet in the Justices' Conference Room. The building also has a law library for legal research.

Workers in protective clothing cleaned the Supreme Court of anthrax in 2001.

A Time of Crisis

In the early 1950s, the case known as *Brown v. Board of Education* became one of the most significant cases in Supreme Court history. The case challenged the Court—and Chief Justice Earl Warren—to decide whether to change long-standing laws that had treated African Americans unfairly.

Chief Justice Earl Warren

Linda Brown, an African American girl from Topeka, Kansas, was forbidden by law to attend a new public school near her home. Only white students could attend. Linda had to walk across a dangerous railroad yard each day and take a bus to a rundown school for black students that was several miles from her home.

In 1951, Linda's father, Reverend Oliver Brown, sued Topeka's Board of Education. He argued that his daughter and other black children should be allowed to attend school with white children. Other African Americans agreed. They said laws that support racial segregation, or separation, of schools were unconstitutional. Many people, however, strongly opposed school desegregation. Finally, *Brown v. Board of Education* was brought before the Supreme Court.

For many years, black students were forced to go to rundown schools because of racial segregation.

Warren believed that prosegregation laws were morally wrong. He also believed such laws violated the 14th Amendment to the Constitution. Under this amendment, each state must provide all citizens equal protection under the laws.

In 1896, the Supreme Court had ruled in a case known as *Plessy v. Ferguson.* That ruling said "separate but equal" facilities were constitutional. Some associate justices in Warren's court argued that the Plessy decision meant whites and blacks could attend separate schools, as long as the schools were of equal quality. Warren argued that separate white and black schools could never actually be equal, because African Americans were treated unfairly in American society.

Thurgood Marshall (center) stands outside of the Supreme Court after winning the Brown *case.*

Warren worked tirelessly to convince the other justices to vote with him. He believed that the Court had a responsibility to vote unanimously—9 to 0—to send a message that segregation was unconstitutional.

In order to gain such a vote, Warren had to make compromises. Justices from southern states were afraid that if desegregation took place too quickly, violence might occur. So Warren agreed not to give a specific deadline for desegregating schools.

On May 17, 1954, the Supreme Court unanimously ruled that segregation of public schools was against the Constitution. Warren had convinced all 8 associate justices to vote with him. As he explained, "Separate educational facilities are inherently [automatically] unequal."

Another Time of Crisis

In 1807, Chief Justice John Marshall presided as a trial judge over the first treason trial in U.S. history. Former vice president Aaron Burr was accused of plotting to create his own empire in the Louisiana Territory, which was owned by the United States. Marshall acquitted Burr because the Constitution declared that all acts of treason had to be witnessed by 2 people and take place within U.S. boundaries. No one had witnessed a specific act by Burr, and while he was hatching his plan, Louisiana was not yet part of the United States. The chief justice was the first legal authority to rule on treason.

A Chief Justice's Day

During the 9 months that the Court is in session, the chief justice's workday is busy. Here is what a day might be like for the chief justice.

6:00 AM   Wake, shower, read newspaper, eat breakfast

7:30 AM   Arrive at chambers; assign tasks to administrative assistants and law clerks

9:00 AM   Lead a private meeting with associate justices to read petitions and decide on cases to accept

10:00 AM Sitting: Preside over 2 courtroom cases

12:00 PM Eat lunch; check in with assistants; make phone calls

People line up outside of the Supreme Court Building for a sitting to begin.

1:00 PM	Sitting: Return to the courtroom to preside over 2 more hearings
3:00 PM	Meet with associate justices to discuss the cases they have heard
5:00 PM	Hold a discussion with students in a college law class
6:30 PM	Dinner; watch television news
8:00 PM	Give speech at a meeting of the American Bar Association
10:00 PM	Return home; read law journals
11:00 PM	Bed

Chief Justice Warren Burger speaks at a lawyers' organization.

Fascinating Facts

President William Howard Taft was the only person to serve as both chief justice of the Supreme Court and president of the United States. He was president from 1909 to 1913, and chief justice from 1921 to 1930. Taft enjoyed being chief justice more than president. As chief justice, he once joked, "I don't remember that I ever was president."

John Jay, the first chief justice, was also the youngest. He was 43 years old when he joined the Supreme Court.

Chief Justice John Jay

The fourth chief justice, **John Marshall**, had the longest term of service. He served from 1801 to 1835, for a total of 34 years and 5 months. Marshall took part in over 1,000 Supreme Court decisions. He was the secretary of state under John Adams, the second president, before being confirmed to the Supreme Court.

John Rutledge had the shortest term of service as chief justice. He served for only 4 months, from August to December 1795.

Chief Justice John Marshall

George Washington, the first president of the United States, appointed 3 chief justices and 7 associate justices, more than any other president.

Supreme Court justices always wear black robes in the courtroom, a tradition that began over 200 years ago. The robe of the chief justice has 4 stripes on each sleeve.

Before their private conferences and courtroom hearings, the 9 justices all shake hands with each other. This tradition symbolizes the fact that the justices are working together toward the common goal of justice.

Chief Justice John Rutledge

Following tradition, quill pens (pens made of feathers) are still placed at the desks in the courtroom today.

Louis Brandeis was the first Jewish Supreme Court justice. He served from 1916 to 1939.

Justice Louis Brandeis

Glossary

amendment—a change or correction made in a government document such as the Constitution

appeal—the act of bringing a case to a higher court for review

appoint—to assign a person to a certain position in the government

cabinet—a council of advisers who help manage the government

case—an argument concerning U.S. laws and the actions of an individual or group

Constitution—the document that established the U.S. government and that contains the principles and laws of the nation

dissenting—the minority or losing side of a court decision

impeachment—the act of removing an elected official from office

justice—a judge or ruling member of the Supreme Court

lectern—the stand behind which a lawyer argues his case

petition—a request submitted for the Supreme Court to hear a case

segregation—the separation of different races or groups of people

sitting—a session in the Supreme Court during which justices gather to hear lawyers present their case

Supreme Court—the highest court or legal assembly which decides the outcomes of legal cases

treason—the act of attempting to overthrow or undermine a government

For More Information

Publications

Quiri, Patricia Ryon. *The Constitution.* Danbury, CT: Children's Press, 1999.

Sanders, Mark S. *The Supreme Court.* Austin, TX: Raintree Steck-Vaughn, 2001.

Web sites

Supreme Court of the United States

http://www.supremecourtus.gov

The official Supreme Court web site. Includes recent opinions, calendar, case handling guides, and court rules.

United States Courts

http://www.uscourts.gov

The Federal Judiciary website. Includes information from and about the U.S. Judicial Branch.

Index